Here, There and Everywhere

Liz Weir

THE O'BRIEN PRESS
DUBLIN

First published 2005 by The O'Brien Press Ltd,
12 Terenure Road East, Rathgar, Dublin 6, Ireland.
Tel: +353 1 4923333; Fax: +353 1 4922777
E-mail: books@obrien.ie
Website: www.obrien.ie
Reprinted 2007.

ISBN: 978-0-86278-869-8

British Library Cataloguing-in-Publication Data
Weir, Liz
Here, there and everywhere: stories from many lands
1.Children's stories, English
I.Title 823.9'14[J]

**2 3 4 5 6 7 8 9 10
07 08 09 10**

The O'Brien Press receives assistance from

Layout and design: The O'Brien Press Ltd
Printing: Cox & Wyman Ltd

Contents

Dedication:

In memory of Nancy DeVries,

a fine storyteller and friend

The Fisherman of Lough Neagh

There was once a fisherman called Seamus who lived on the shores of Lough Neagh, in County Antrim. Now, the lough is so big it's like a sea, and in the wintertime when the wind blows, the water gets so rough that you can hardly take a boat out on it. When he couldn't go fishing, Seamus would earn money to keep his family by chopping wood.

But that winter had been very long and bitter, and now there were hardly any trees left. One cold, crisp morning, as Seamus walked along the lough shore, he saw a branch of a tree hanging out over the water. Taking his axe, he clambered out and started to chop the wood. But his hands were so cold that the axe slipped from his fingers, down into the deep, dark water.

Seamus knew he could never get his axe back; the lough was too deep. How could he ever afford another one? He put his head down

in his hands and started to sob. All
of a sudden he heard a voice say,
'What's wrong?'

Seamus looked in the direction of
the water and saw a tiny boat, no
bigger than one of his boots. Sitting
in the boat was a little fisherman,
with a tiny fishing rod and line. It
was a fairy man.

'I've lost my axe,' said Seamus.

'Have you indeed?' said the little
man. 'Would you like me to try and
find it for you?'

'Oh, please!' said Seamus, who
always minded his manners.

So the little man cast out his line, and within a minute he was reeling in an axe. But to Seamus's amazement, it was made of solid gold.

'Is this your axe?' said the wee man.

'No,' said Seamus, 'my axe wasn't made of gold.'

'I'll try again,' said the little man. He cast out his line again, and when he reeled it in there was another axe, but this one was made of silver.

'Is this your axe?' asked the little man.

'No,' said Seamus, 'sure, my axe wasn't made of silver.'

'Third time lucky,' said the little man, casting out his line. Sure enough, when he reeled it in, there was Seamus's axe.

'Oh, thank you, thank you,' said Seamus, as the man brought his tiny boat to the shore. But when Seamus looked down, there at the water's edge were his own axe, the silver axe and the gold axe. Seamus gasped. The little man turned to Seamus and said, 'You are an honest man, and honesty should always be rewarded, Seamus.' With that, the tiny fisherman disappeared.

Seamus gathered up the axes. He went to the market. He sold the gold one and the silver one for a great price, and of course the news spread all around the village.

Now, there was a man in the village called Michael who was a bit sneaky, and thought this might be an excellent way to make himself rich. So, taking an old rusty saw, he went to the same spot, at the same time of day. He leaned out and pretended to saw the branch, but all of a sudden Michael just threw his rusty old saw down into the water. Then he sat back, put his head in his hands and pretended to cry – big sobs, all the while casting his eye round and about to see if anyone was looking at him, which is a thing you should always do if you're pretending to cry.

All of a sudden he heard a voice say, 'What's wrong with you?' He looked up and, sure enough, there was the wee man. He was exactly as Seamus had described him, in a boat no bigger than a boot, with his tiny rod and tiny line.

'I've lost my saw,' sobbed Michael.

'Have you indeed?' said the little man. 'I suppose you want me to find it for you?'

'Yes!' Michael didn't even say please.

The tiny fisherman sighed. He cast out his line and, when he reeled it in, there on the end was a gleaming golden saw. Michael gasped.

'Is this your saw?' asked the wee man.

'Oh, yes it is,' said Michael.

'Indeed it is not!' said the fairy man.

'You know as well as I do your saw wasn't made of gold.' And with that, the saw, the fairy man and the boat simply vanished into thin air, and Michael never saw any of them again.

Seamus and his family lived happily from that day. As for Michael, he had to go and buy himself a brand new saw. And do you know something? It served him right for being so greedy!

The Lion and
the Rabbit

Long ago in Africa there was a very fierce lion. Every day he went out hunting. He would catch and eat animal after animal. That's what lions have always done, just like you or I might go for a take-away.

Years passed and the lion became very old and very stiff. He could no longer run fast to catch his prey.

One night he called all the animals together for a big meeting. He roared to get them to pay attention.

'From now on,' he said in a huge, booming voice, 'every night at six o'clock, one of you has to come to my cave so that I can eat you. You decide who it's going to be.' And away he walked.

The animals all stood around wondering what to do.

'Any volunteers?' asked the elephant. 'Who wants to be eaten?'

'Not me!' said the zebra.

'Not me!' said the antelope.

All the animals shuffled about nervously for a while. Then they did something that even people do sometimes. They started to argue with each other. Then they started pointing and whispering.

'What about those animals over there? They're not like us.'

'How about them? They're smaller than we are.'

'They're fatter!'

'They can't run as fast as we can!'

'They're a different colour!'

In the end the animals all picked

on the oldest, smelliest, plumpest rabbit they could find. He was not a happy bunny. But the others had all chosen him, so he had to go.

The rabbit hopped slowly towards the lion's cave. When he was halfway there, he saw a wishing well. He decided to drop in a stone and make a wish, just in case.

As he leaned over the well he saw his reflection in the water. Suddenly he had a very good idea. He dropped the stone into the water and made a big wish.

By the time he got to the lion's cave the lion was furious.

'What kept you?' he roared. 'You're late!'

'Sorry about that,' said the rabbit. 'On my way here I met another lion and he said he was King of the Jungle!'

'What?' snarled the lion. '*I'm* King of the Jungle!'

'I told him that,' said the rabbit, 'but he said he was going to eat me.'

'What?' roared the lion. '*I'm* going to eat you!'

'That's what I tried to tell him before I ran away,' explained the rabbit.

'Where is he?' The lion was really angry now.

'Follow me,' said the rabbit. 'I'll show you.'

The rabbit led the way slowly back to the wishing well. When they got there the rabbit pointed down inside the well and whispered, 'He's down there. I can't look, I'm too scared.'

'Scared?' roared the lion. 'Well, I'm not scared!'

The lion leaned over the well and ROARED!

A quieter echo roared back.

'Who are you?' roared the lion.

'Who are *you*?' the echo replied.

'I'm the King of the Jungle!' roared the lion.

'*I'm* the King of the Jungle,' the echo replied.

'No, you're not,' roared the lion. 'I am.'

'No, you're not, *I* am!' the echo replied.

'I'm going to get you!' roared the lion.

'I'm going to get *you*!' the echo replied.

With that, the lion jumped down into the well. There was a big splash and then silence.

The old rabbit hopped back to the other animals. They were surprised to see him.

'You're alive!' gasped the zebra.

'The lion didn't eat you up?' asked the antelope.

'No,' said the rabbit, 'and I don't think the lion will eat anyone else.'

Then all the animals realised something very important,

something that people should also remember. Never pick on anyone else, because sometimes you can get a really big surprise!

How the Snow got its Colour

Long ago, when the world was new, everything was given a colour. The sky was blue; the grass was green; the soil was brown. There was only one thing that had no colour at all, and that was the snow. The snow was clear – you could see right through it! When snow fell, it looked just like rain. When it was snowing, people would say, 'Does it ever stop raining around here?' Imagine making a see-through snowman!

The snow looked around, and saw that flowers had many different colours. So first of all the snow went up to a red rose and said, 'Excuse me, red rose, would you give me some of your colour?'

'What?' said the rose. 'You want some of my red?'

'Yes, yes, if you could give me some of your colour, wouldn't I look lovely? People would look out through their windows and see red snowflakes coming down. They would build red snow-men and throw red snowballs.'

'Oh, go away!' said the red rose. 'When people see me, they think of summer, they think of warmth.

They don't think of cold and wind.'

So the snow thought he would try another flower. He went over to a beautiful yellow daffodil and said, 'Oh, daffodil, you look so pretty. Your colour is so bright and beautiful. Could you give me a little of your yellow?'

The daffodil said, 'What?'

'Please,' said the snow. 'I would look so lovely. People would look out and trees would be covered in yellow and there would be yellow on all the rooftops. It would be so beautiful.'

'Go away!' said the daffodil. 'When people see me they know that winter is over, and that spring is here. Just go away.'

The snow had almost given up, when he noticed a tiny white flower poking up out of the ground.

'Oh, hello, white flower,' he said. 'Your colour is so clean and fresh. If you could give me some of your white, the whole world would look different in winter. People would see the white glow and know it had been snowing even before they opened their curtains in the morning.

Everything would look crisp and new.'

The little flower said, 'Do you know what? I think you're right.' She reached up and scraped a tiny piece of white from her head.

She threw it at the snow and … *shhooo*! Lovely white flakes of snow began to fall.

Oh! The snow was so delighted.

'Little flower,' he said, 'you've been so kind to me, now let me be kind to you. From this day on, no matter how cold it gets, the frost will never nip your blossoms.

Even when the ground is frozen hard, you will be the first flower of the spring to push its way up through the soil.'

Ever since then, that flower has been called the snowdrop. Next time you see a snowdrop, look up underneath it. You will see a little piece of green, and that is where the snowdrop scraped off her colour and gave it to the snow.

The Mermaid's Gift

Mary and Bridget lived beside each other in Donegal, but they were not at all alike. Mary was the sort of girl who always did as she was told, but Bridget wasn't. If Bridget's mother told her to be home by six, she might come home at half-past six. If her mother told her to wear a red dress, Bridget would wear a blue one. But they were still the best of friends.

One day they were playing on the rocks near the beach when Mary said, 'Come on, Bridget, it's time we were getting home.'

'No, not yet,' said Bridget.

'Well, I'm going home,' said Mary, and she started to climb up the rocks.

Just then she stopped, and said, 'Listen, can you hear it?'

'Hear what?' said Bridget. 'I thought you were in a hurry.'

'Just listen,' whispered Mary.

Lovely singing was drifting on the wind from behind a rock.

Both girls looked over and saw a beautiful lady, in a dress that was all the colours of the sea – greens, blues and silvery greys. She wore a necklace of seashells, and seaweed was plaited into her hair. Mary and Bridget gasped when they saw she had a silvery tail. She was a mermaid.

Mary spoke first: 'You've a lovely voice.'

'Indeed you have,' said Bridget quickly.

The mermaid jumped with shock. But when she saw the girls meant

her no harm, she sat back down and sang a long song of the sea. It was both sad and happy at the same time, a song of shipwreck and rescue and the mysteries of the deep.

The sun was going down and the girls could see the light glinting off jewels in the mermaid's lap – rings, brooches and earrings. Then she stopped singing and said, 'It's time you girls were going home. I want to give each of you a gift to take with you.'

The mermaid lifted two bags that looked like spun silver and into each she put pearls, rubies and diamonds, treasure from the sea.

'These gifts must be shared with all your family. Don't stop till you get home, and remember to share what is in the bag.'

'Thank you,' Mary whispered breathlessly.

Bridget was already on the path. 'Oh, yeah … thanks!' she called back over her shoulder.

When the two of them were half-way home, Bridget stopped.

'There's nothing in this bag,' she said. 'It feels empty.'

'Will you come on,' said Mary. 'The mermaid said we were not to stop.'

But it was too late. Bridget had opened the bag. She tipped it up and out came nothing but a stream of fine silver sand.

'See, I told you,' she said. 'It's a trick! Come on, open yours.'

Mary took to her heels and ran for home, not stopping once. She ran into the house and there sitting at the table were her mother, her granny and her little brother. Her daddy was out at sea, fishing.

Mary tipped up the bag and out fell all the precious jewels. The family were amazed. They decided to share the gift. First, they bought a new fishing boat for their daddy and his two brothers. Then they built a restaurant high on the cliff top, where they cooked all the fish that were caught. The restaurant soon became famous for miles around. It was called 'The Mermaid's Gift', for that was what it had been.

The Three Bears Rap

*Start by clapping your hands and
knees to get the rhythm going!*

Once upon a time in the nursery rhyme there were three bears.
I said three bears!
One was a Mama bear, one was a
Papa bear and one was a wee bear!
A wee bear!
They all went a-walking in the
deep woods a-talking,

when along came a little girl with long flowing golden hair.

What was her name?

Goldilocks!

She knocked on the door and no-one was there so she walked on in.

Along came the three bears.

'Someone's been eating my porridge!' said the Papa Bear.

Said the Papa bear (arms folded, cross face, deep voice)

'Someone's been eating my porridge!' said the Mama Bear.

Said the Mama bear (hands on hips)

'Hey, Mama, see there!' said
the little wee bear,

'Someone has broken my
chair!' *Huh! (hands in the air)*

'Someone has broken my chair!'
Huh! (hands in the air)

'Someone's been sitting in my
chair!' said the Papa Bear.

Said the Papa bear (arms folded,
cross face, deep voice)

'Someone's been sitting in my
chair!' said the Mama Bear.

Said the Mama bear (hands on hips)

'Hey, Mama, see there!' said
the little wee bear,

'Someone has broken my chair!' *Huh! (hands in the air)*

'Someone has broken my chair!' Huh! (hands in the air)

'Someone's been sleeping in my bed!' said the Papa Bear.

Said the Papa bear (arms folded, cross face, deep voice)

'Someone's been sleeping in my bed!' said the Mama Bear.

Said the Mama bear (hands on hips)

'Hey, Mama, see there!' said the little wee bear,

'Someone has broken my chair!' *Huh! (hands in the air)*

'*Someone has broken my chair!*'
Huh! (hands in the air)

Goldilocks woke up and broke
up the party,
And she ran out of there.
And she ran out of there.

'Bye, bye, bye, bye, bye, bye,
bye!' said the Papa Bear.

'*Bye, bye, bye, bye, bye, bye, bye!*'
said the Papa bear (arms folded,
cross face, deep voice)

'Bye, bye, bye, bye, bye, bye,
bye,' said the Mama Bear.

'*Bye, bye, bye, bye, bye, bye, bye!*'
said the Mama bear (hands on hips)

'Hey Mama, see there!' said the little wee bear.

And that's the story of the Three Bears Rap!

Huh!

Why the Sky
is Far Away

A long time ago in Africa, the sky was so close you could touch it. Better than that, you could break bits off it to eat. The sky would come in any flavour you wanted. If you felt like some chocolate, or some cheese, or some chicken, there it was. This meant that animals did not have to be killed for people to eat, and they

were happy about that. It also meant that no matter how much rain there was, or how hot it became, there was always enough for people to eat, and nobody went hungry.

Some people were greedy though, and broke off great big bits of sky. Sometimes the bits were so big that they couldn't even eat them and they just threw the leftovers on rubbish heaps. The rubbish heaps got higher and higher.

One night there was a terrible

thunderstorm. It woke all the people up. They heard a loud and terrible voice:

'Tell your people to stop wasting me! If they don't stop wasting me they will see what will happen.'

They knew this was the voice of the sky.

For a while after that, the people were very careful. They broke off tiny bits of sky and nibbled them slowly. As time went on, however, they became careless again.

One night a woman was coming home from a big feast. She started thinking about all that she had eaten and started feeling hungry again. Without thinking, she reached up and broke off a huge piece of sky. After eating a bit of it she knew she could not finish it. She called to her children and they ate a little, but it was no good, there was still a big piece of sky left. She threw it on the rubbish heap. It was dark, she thought to herself, and no-one would notice.

That night there was a great thunderstorm. It roared and crashed all night. All the people woke up, but no

voice came. They were very re-
lieved.

The next morning when the
people went outside, they felt the
hot sun burning down on their
heads. They looked up and there,
far above them, was the distant
blue sky. And that is where the sky
has stayed ever since.

Noah's Ark

Long ago, when a great flood covered the earth, Noah loaded all the animals two by two on to his Ark to save them until the water went down.

After a few days, Noah noticed a hole in the side of the Ark. Water was coming in through it.

'I need help!' called Noah. 'Elephant, you're big, can you do something?'

Elephant went over to the hole and put his trunk on it, but the water came up his trunk and made him cough.

'I can't do it!' he spluttered. 'There's water up my nose!'

Next came Monkey. 'Oooh, oooh, oooh! Let me try!' he screeched.

Monkey sat down on the place where the water was coming in. He soon jumped up again!

'It's too cold,' he moaned. 'I don't have enough fur on that bit of me to keep warm.'

Just then, Dog came over.

'Let me try, Noah,' he barked. 'I think I can help.'

Dog very quietly went and put his nose into the hole. He kept it there for the rest of the voyage.

At last the Ark reached dry land and all the animals came off. Noah turned to dog and said, 'Thanks for saving us. From now on you shall be known as man's best friend.'

Just then they all noticed something about dog's nose – it had been in the hole so long that it was all wet and cold. And that's how dogs' noses have remained from that day to this!

Mother Owl's Revenge

Long ago in the forests of America there lived an animal that was covered from head to toe in long, silky, white fur. He was a terribly vain creature and as he passed a pond he would stop to admire himself. He thought he was very beautiful.

One day, as he was walking through the forest, the creature felt hungry. He looked up and saw a mother owl flying out of her nest. He knew that would mean she had left her chicks. This could be a handy meal for him.

He climbed up the tree and came to the nest. Inside were three baby owls. He lifted one out and held it up to have a look at it.

'Eugh!' he said. 'You are so ugly and I am so lovely. I couldn't eat you!'

He dropped the baby owl back into the nest and climbed back down the tree.

A few minutes later the mother owl flew back with a mouth full of tasty grubs and worms for her babies. All she could hear was them making a terrible noise.

'What's wrong?' she asked. 'Who has upset you like this? Tell Mummy what happened.'

In between tiny cries the first little owl gulped, 'An animal came and he said we were ugly!'

'What?' said his mother. 'He said you were ugly? He said my babies were ugly? You are beautiful! Tell Mummy who said this to you.'

'It was an animal with white fur,' said the little owl.

'That does not surprise me,' said the mother owl. 'You babies eat up your worms and I'll be back soon.'

The mother owl was really angry as she swooped low over the trees. She knew who she was looking for. That creature needed to be taught some manners. How dare he say nasty things about her babies!

With her keen eyes she soon spotted the animal with the white fur. She snatched him up in her sharp talons and carried him high

above the trees. Just then she saw
the remains of an old bonfire far
below. It gave her a very good idea.

The mother owl swooped low and
dragged the animal through the
black ashes of the fire. She then
turned and pulled him back
through it on the other side. Then
she dropped him into a pond.

The mother owl watched as the
creature pulled himself out of the
water. He looked quite different.
From the tip of his nose to the tip
of his tail on one side, his fur has
been singed black. From the tip of

his nose to the tip of his tail on the other side, his fur had been singed black. Only down the middle of his back was there a narrow stripe of white.

Ever since then, that animal has been known as a skunk. The thing that most people know about the skunk is that he has a horrible smell. That's the smell of the burnt fur as he was pulled through the bonfire and it's still with him to this day!

The King with Horse's Ears

Once there was a very bold prince. Because his daddy was the King and his mummy was the Queen, he was totally spoilt. He could do almost anything he liked. He called people names, he teased other children and he was mean to animals. Nobody ever gave out to him.

One day the prince was strolling

through the palace stables when, for no reason at all, he lifted his foot and kicked one of the royal horses.

He thought no-one saw him, but there in the corner of the stable was an old woman dressed in a black cloak. She decided the prince must be taught a lesson, once and for all. And she had the power to do it.

The next morning, when the prince woke up, he felt very strange. He lifted up one hand to the top of his head and felt something there.

He lifted up the other hand and felt something else. He jumped out of bed to look in the mirror. There, on top of his head, were two horse's ears!

What was he to do? He couldn't run and say, 'Mummy, Daddy, I kicked one of your horses and now I have horse's ears!'

He decided he would keep it a secret. He would hide the ears under his crown.

From then on the prince was never seen without his crown. He wore it when he was playing, he wore it in the bath, he even wore it in bed. Everybody in the palace thought it was a bit odd but, since he was so much quieter and better behaved, nobody passed any remarks about it.

Years passed and the prince became king. He married and had children of his own. But, during all those years, no-one ever saw him without his crown. No-one, that is, except for the royal barber, as princes and kings and people of quality need to keep their hair looking smart. The king made the

barber promise never to tell anyone his secret, or else he would have his head cut off. In those days kings could do that sort of thing.

The barber kept the secret for years and years. Now, it is very hard to keep such a big secret for such a long time. The barber couldn't stop thinking about the King's ears, but he couldn't tell anyone about them. He couldn't sleep properly; he couldn't eat properly. He was very unhappy. At last he went to the doctor, who checked him out and said,

'I can find nothing the matter with you. Are you worrying about something?'

'I can't tell you,' said the barber.

'Well,' said the doctor, 'If you can't tell me, why don't you take a walk in the forest and tell it to the trees?'

The barber took a walk that very evening. He found a very big tree in the middle of the forest with a hole in its trunk.

He got right up close to it and whispered, 'The King has horse's ears!'

Whew! He'd said it out loud. What a relief! He felt so much better.

Just about this time the King was planning a big birthday party. He had invited all the other kings and queens and all the important people from round about to join in the fun. He ordered the cooks to prepare the best of food. He wanted to have some fine music for his party, so he called for the royal harper.

'It's time you made yourself a new harp,' ordered the King. 'Go into the forest and pick any tree you like. Only the best will do.'

The next day the harper went deep into the forest and chose a fine, strong tree. He made himself a beautiful new harp out of it.

On the day of the party all the guests were gathered in the royal palace. The King and Queen and the royal children were dressed in their grandest clothes and the King was wearing a wonderful new crown.

The order was given: 'And now, let the royal music start!'

The moment the royal harper plucked the strings of his brand new harp, it began to sing, 'The King has horse's ears, the King has horse's ears!'

Everyone stared at the King. First he turned pale. Then he turned red. Then he turned purple. Giggling and whispering started in the crowd, and spread throughout the palace.

'That's why he wears his crown all the time. He's got horse's ears!'

The King lost his temper and pulled the crown off his head.

'All right, have a laugh,' he shouted. Up popped two horse's ears!

The crowd roared with laughter and tears started to roll down the King's cheeks.

Then the Queen spoke. 'Stop this at once!' she said. 'This is your King and my husband! He's been a good king. He's a good husband and a good father to our children. I rather like his ears. I think they look quite special.'

Then the crowd grew silent. People started saying kind things about the King and his ears.

'Actually, they look quite smart … Well, they are different …'

From then on, the King some-times wore his crown, and some-times he didn't. He was happy.

There was one even happier person in the kingdom though. That was the barber, because he had realised that a secret is better out than in!

Also by Liz Weir:

Boom Chicka Boom

Available in book and CD form.
Nine stories – old and new – with participation rhymes and
playful verses. Full of magic and drama.

Book ISBN 978-0-86278-417-1
CD ISBN 978-0-86278-470-6

Praise for *Boom Chicka Boom:*

'The wonderful storyteller Liz Weir creates a lovely little
collection of stories and rhymes in *Boom Chicka Boom*
which makes a most welcome reappearance.'
The School Librarian

'The format of this book makes it an ideal reader
for 5-8 year olds although it would be useful on the
pre-school book shelf to read at story-time.'
Books Books Books

'Nine magical stories told with gusto ... Adults will rediscover
the pleasurable terror and word play of childhood and be just
as enthralled as younger readers'
The Sunday Independent

Here, There and Everywhere

Also available in CD form

Liz Weir uses all of her experience
and skill as a storyteller to bring
the stories from *Here, There and
Everywhere* to life with her lively
and fun reading of the text.

ISBN 978-0-86278-895-7

What's on www.obrien.ie?

➢ detailed information on all
O'Brien Press books,
both current and forthcoming

➢ sample chapters from many books

➢ author information

➢ book reviews by other readers

➢ authors writing about their own books

➢ teachers' and students' thoughts about
author visits to their schools

What are you waiting for?
Check out www.obrien.ie today.